George Meade

MILITARY LEADERS OF THE CIVIL WAR

Don McLeese

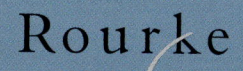

Rourke
Publishing LLC
Vero Beach, Florida 32964

© 2006 Rourke Publishing LLC

All rights reserved. No part of this book may be reproduced or utilized in any form or by any means, electronic or mechanical including photocopying, recording, or by any information storage and retrieval system without permission in writing from the publisher.

www.rourkepublishing.com

PHOTO CREDITS: P06 ©Getty Images
all other images Library of Congress

Title page: General George Meade meets with his staff in Virginia.

Editor: Frank Sloan

Cover and page design by Nicola Stratford

Library of Congress Cataloging-in-Publication Data

McLeese, Don.
 George Meade / Don McLeese.
  p. cm. -- (Military leaders of the civil war)
 Includes index.
 ISBN 1-59515-480-9 (hardcover)
 1. Meade, George Gordon, 1815-1872--Juvenile literature. 2. Generals--United States--Biography--Juvenile literature. 3. United States. Army--Biography--Juvenile literature. 4. United States--History--Civil War, 1861-1865--Campaigns--Juvenile literature. I. Title.
 E467.1.M38M29 2006
 973.7'349'092--dc22

2005010985

Printed in the USA

Rourke Publishing
1-800-394-7055
www.rourkepublishing.com
sales@rourkepublishing.com
Post Office Box 3328, Vero Beach, FL 32964

Table of Contents

The Winning General at Gettysburg 4

Born in Spain 7

Different Schools 8

West Point 11

In the Army 12

Off to Florida 15

Sick and Tired 16

Working on the Railroad 19

A Married Man 20

Planning Lighthouses 22

The Civil War 24

Taking Charge 26

Victory at Gettysburg 29

Important Dates to Remember 30

Glossary 31

Index 32

Further Reading/Websites to Visit 32

The Winning General at Gettysburg

~

From July 1 through July 3 in 1863, the North and the South fought one of the most important battles of the Civil War. The battle took place near a small town in southern Pennsylvania called Gettysburg. In the Battle of Gettysburg, the **Union** army of the North had 90,000 **soldiers** and the **Confederate** army of the South had 75,000.

The leader of the Union **troops** was Major **General** George Gordon Meade. Though he was new to his job, he was ready. When General Robert E. Lee, the head of the Confederate army, led his troops into Pennsylvania, the Union turned them back.

The Battle of Gettysburg made Major General Meade famous for winning one of the most important victories in the Civil War.

The Battle of Gettysburg was considered a major turning point in the war. After losing this battle, the South surrendered the next year.

*General Meade on horseback at Gettysburg.
Despite his birth in Spain, Meade was an American from the start.*

Born in Spain

George Gordon Meade was born on December 31, 1815. Almost all of the soldiers who fought in the Civil War were born in America. But George wasn't. His family had moved to the country of **Spain**. His parents were living at the time in the Spanish city of Cadiz. George's father was named Richard Meade, and he was a businessman. He was also working with the U. S. navy. George's mother was named Margaret Coates Meade.

Both of his parents were **citizens** of the United States. They left Spain and returned to the United States not long after George was born.

Spain: This is one of the major countries in Europe, across the Atlantic Ocean from the United States. The language spoken there is Spanish.

Different Schools

~

The first American city where George lived with his family was Philadelphia, in Pennsylvania. George's father had some business and money problems. George first went to Mt. Airy School in Philadelphia, but he had to leave because his father didn't have enough money. The family moved to Baltimore and later lived in Washington, D.C., when George was a boy. He went to many different schools.

Philadelphia is one of the oldest and most important cities in America. It is sometimes called the birthplace of the United States.

Meade trained at West Point to become an officer.

West Point

~

Though he had to switch schools a lot, George was a very good student. He wanted to go to a regular college, but his parents wanted him to go to the U.S. **Military** Academy. This was at West Point in New York.

The school known as West Point was a good college, and those who went there didn't have to pay anything. Instead, they trained to be military officers, and they promised to serve in the army after college. In 1831, George went to West Point and started college at the academy.

Cadets: Students at military academies are called cadets. They are students who are training to be army officers.

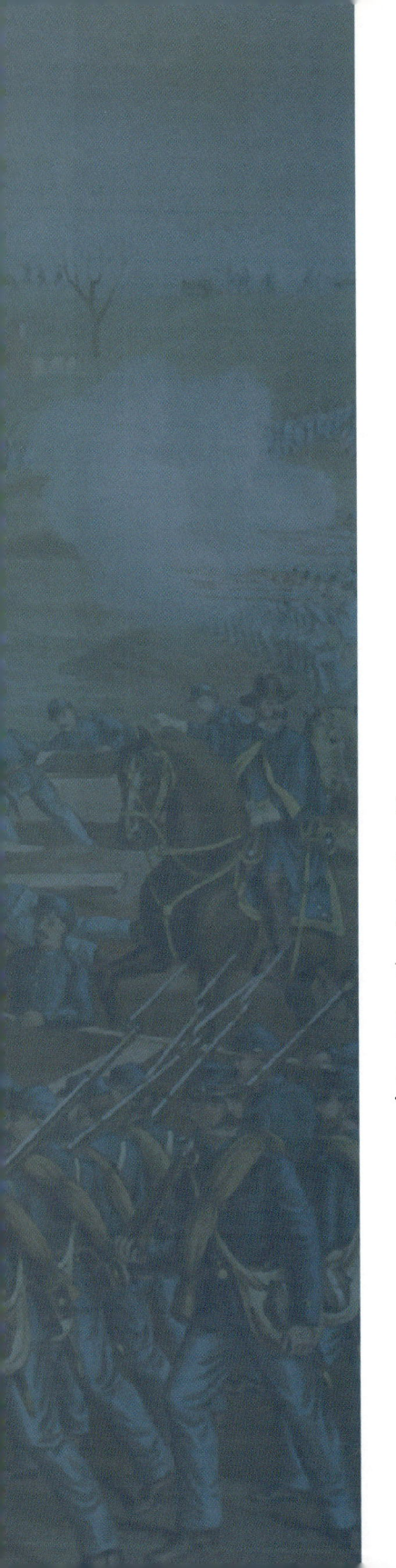

In the Army

~

At West Point, George liked his regular classes rather than training to become an officer. He didn't really want to join the military, but he knew he had to. He was one of the best students when he graduated in 1835. He was nineteenth in his class. He was given the rank of lieutenant and joined the **artillery**.

A photograph of cannons taken during the Civil War

The Seminole Wars lasted from 1835 until 1842.

Off to Florida

~

When George left West Point, the U.S. Army was beginning to fight a tribe of Native Americans in Florida called the **Seminoles**. The United States thought the Seminoles should move away from Florida, but the tribe wanted to stay there. George was sent to Florida at the start of the Seminole Wars in 1835.

Seminole Wars: Most of the Seminoles agreed to move west, but some stayed. In the 1850s there was a later war between the United States and those Seminoles who remained in Florida.

Sick and Tired

~

When George was in Florida, he became very sick with a bad fever. He was so sick he couldn't fight the war. The army let him leave Florida to go north to Massachusetts. Instead of being in battle, he would work at an army office. George had never really wanted to be in the army. Being sick made him even more tired of being a soldier. He decided to quit the army in 1836.

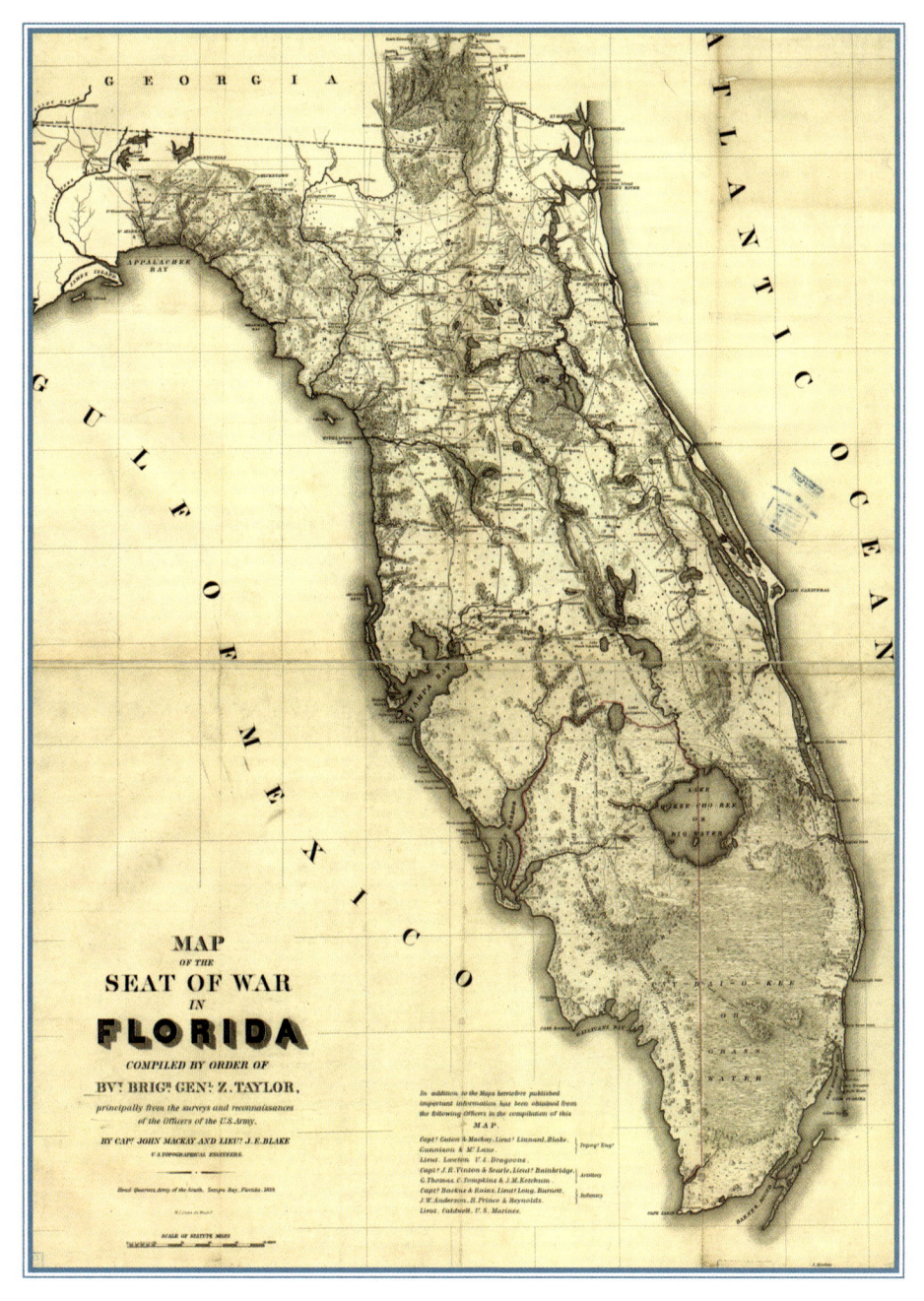

A map of Florida that dates from 1839

The railroad bridge shown here is the kind of project that resulted from Meade's engineering skills.

18

Working on the Railroad

George then went to work for a railroad company. His job was to draw maps of territory and plans for where to put new railroad tracks. He would go into those areas and **survey** them. He was called an **engineer**. He liked this better than being in the army.

Railroad engineers: On a railroad, the person who drives the train is also called an "engineer." This word has two different meanings. George wasn't that kind of engineer. He was the type who surveyed.

A Married Man

~

While he was working for the railroad, George fell in love with a woman named Margaretta Sergeant. She lived in Washington, D.C. They met in 1840 and married soon afterward.

Now that he was a married man, George wanted to make more money than he could with the railroad. In 1842, he decided to join the army again, only this time as an engineer. Just like the railroad, the army need engineers to look at territory and draw maps and plans.

A group of engineers surveys for a railroad.

Planning Lighthouses

~

Because he was in the army, Meade had to fight in wars. In 1845, he was sent to Texas when the United States was at war with Mexico. Parts of what are now Texas and California were then part of Mexico. Once the Mexican War ended in 1848, George returned to live with his wife in Philadelphia. His job for the army was to survey places along the ocean to build lighthouses.

Meade fought at the Battle of Monterey during the Mexican War.

George spent about ten years surveying. He helped to plan where lighthouses would be built and how they would look. He not only surveyed land near the Atlantic Ocean for lighthouses, but he also traveled west to help build lighthouses along the Great Lakes.

Meade helped plan lighthouses that warned ships when dangerous rocks and land might be a hazard.

The Civil War

~

George was still surveying the Great Lakes when the Civil War started in 1861. He went back east to train with his troops near Washington, D.C. He was part of a number of battles in the area against the Confederate army. In one of them, at Glendale, Meade was shot and wounded. He got better in time to fight at the Second Battle of Bull Run, which the Union army lost to the South.

The Great Lakes: These are a chain of the country's largest lakes. They are made up of Lake Superior, Lake Michigan, Lake Huron, Lake Erie, and Lake Ontario.

Meade commanded a division of Union troops at the Battle of Fredericksburg.

Taking Charge

In 1863, just three days before the Battle of Gettysburg, Meade became head of the Army of the Potomac, a part of the Union army. He took over from General Joseph Hooker. This general had also been wounded in battle. Some said he wasn't doing a very good job at leading his troops into war.

Meade took command from General Hooker.

The Potomac River: It runs past Maryland, Virginia, and West Virginia and through Washington, D.C.

General George Meade didn't really want to become head of the Army of the Potomac, but he knew this was his duty. General Robert E. Lee was leading the Southern army into Pennsylvania, and the North had to stop him!

*Generals of the Army of the Potomac.
Meade is shown seated third from the left in the photograph.*

Meade led his troops at the Battle of Gettysburg.

Victory at Gettysburg

The Battle of Gettysburg was one of the hardest fought in the war. Lee's Southern army kept attacking, trying to break through. Meade's Northern army had more soldiers, and they wouldn't let the Southern army through. By July 3, almost 45,000 soldiers were dead, wounded, or captured.

Lee knew he had lost, so he took his troops South into Virginia. Some thought that Meade's Northern troops should have followed them and kept fighting. But Meade had won a big battle, and he thought he'd lost enough men.

After the war, Meade stayed in the army. He died on November 6, 1872, in Philadelphia.

The Gettysburg Address: On November 19, 1863, President Lincoln gave one of the most famous speeches in American history. He gave the speech at Gettysburg, to honor those who had fought and died there.

Important Dates to Remember

1815   George Gordon Meade is born in Spain.

1831   George goes to West Point.

1835   George finishes at West Point and goes to Florida to fight the Seminoles.

1836   George leaves the army and goes to work for the railroad.

1842   After marrying Margaretta Sergeant, George returns to the army.

1845-1848   George fights in the Mexican War.

1861   The Civil War starts. George goes to battle after ten years of surveying for lighthouses.

1863   George leads the Union troops to victory at the Battle of Gettysburg.

1865   The Civil War ends.

1872   George Meade dies.

Glossary

artillery (ar TILL uh ree) — the part of the army that uses cannons and firearms

citizens (SIT uh zenz) — natives of a place who owe allegiance to a government and are entitled to protection from it

Confederate (kon FED ur et) — a person, state, or soldier on the Southern side in the Civil War

engineer (en jin EAR) — someone who makes plans and maps to measure and build.

general (JEN ur ul) — the highest rank in the military

military (MILL ih TARE ee) — the armed forces

Seminoles (SEHM ih nolz) — members of a Native American tribe

soldiers (SOHL jerz) — people who serve in the military

Spain (SPAYN) — a country across the Atlantic Ocean in Europe

survey (SIR vay) — to explore and make a map or a plan

troops (TRUUPS) — soldiers

Union (YOON yun) — the Northern side in the Civil War

Index

Army of the Potomac 26-27
Bull Run, Second Battle of 24
Florida 15-17
Fredericksburg, Battle of 25
Gettysburg, Battle of 4-6, 26, 29
Gettysburg Address 29
Great Lakes 23-24
Lee, Robert E. 27, 29
Meade, Margaret Coates 7
Meade. Richard 7
Mexican War 22
Philadelphia 8-9
Seminole Wars 14-15
U.S. Military Academy (West Point) 10-12
Washington, D.C. 8, 20

Further Reading

Adelson, Bruce. *George Gordon Meade* (Famous Figures of the Civil War Era), Chelsea House, 2001.
Rafuse, Ethan Sepp. *George Gordon Meade and the War in the East,* McWhiney Foundation Press, 2003.
Sauers, Richard A. *Meade: Victor of Gettysburg,* Brassey's, Inc., 2004

Websites To Visit

http://www.nps.gov/gett/getttour/sidebar/meadebio.htm
http://www.ehistory.com/uscw/features/people/bio.cfm?PID=52
http://www.swcivilwar.com/meade.html

About The Author

Don McLeese is an associate professor of journalism at the University of Iowa. He has won many awards for his journalism, and his work has appeared in numerous newspapers and magazines. He has frequently contributed to the World Book Encyclopedia and has written many books for young readers. He lives with his wife and two daughters in West Des Moines, Iowa.

JUN 2 1 2011
2850